The
Raising and Care
of
Guinea Pigs

A Complete Guide to the Breeding
Feeding, Housing, Exhibiting
and Marketing of Cavies

by
A. C. SMITH

Published by
A. C. SMITH
712 West 74th Street
KANSAS CITY, MISSOURI

CONTENTS

Guinea Pigs or Cavies

GUINEA PIGS

CHAPTER I

INTRODUCTION.

The Guinea Pig or Cavy belongs to the rabbit family and is a native of South America. Why they are called Guinea Pigs, no one seems to know, unless their shape suggests a small pig and the name Guinea is a corruption of Guiana, a country in South America. In size, shape and texture of fur they resemble a squirrel or rabbit. They have large bodies, short legs, small feet, no tails and a wide range of colors. A full grown Cavy weighs between two and three pounds, which weight it attains at about 18 months of age. The males are usually larger than the females.

When white people first visited the Andean region of South America they found the Cavy domesticated and living in the houses of the Indians, by whom they were used for food. They were introduced into Europe in the 16th Century and since that time have spread all over the world. In South America there are still several species of wild Cavies. These are hunted as game and are considered a great delicacy.

Cavies are wholly vegetarian in diet, eating about

the same things as a rabbit. They are very easily tamed, are very healthy and hardy, are not noisy, are clean in their habits, and have no offensive odor. There is probably no animal in the world that is easier to handle. They easily adapt themselves to conditions and seem to do equally as well in city or country, in large or small quarters and a few of them together do as well as a large number of them.

They are practically free from the diseases and epidemics that make the raising of poultry and rabbits so uncertain. Some of them get sick and die, of course, but it is usually due to some local cause or to the fact that they have been neglected or improperly fed or housed, but contagious diseases such as will often wipe out whole flocks of poultry or a pen of rabbits are unknown among Cavies.

All of these things make the raising of Guinea Pigs a very pleasant as well as a very profitable occupation.

CHAPTER II

VARIETIES.

English.

There are several varieties of Cavies, distinguished mainly by their fur. The ones most commonly raised and most widely known are the English or smooth-haired. These are the ones you should raise for commercial purposes. They may be in

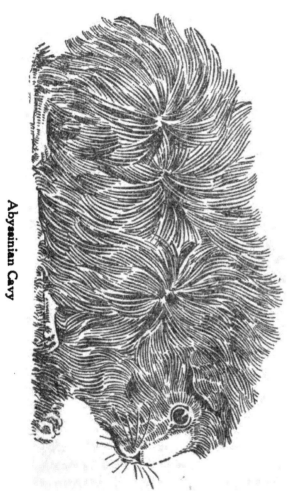

Abyssinian Cavy

color: white, black, red, fawn, cream, gray, brindle, brown, or a mixture of these colors. The whites are usually albinos and have pink eyes.

Peruvian.

The Peruvian has long silken hair and may be called the aristocrat of Cavydom. They are raised principally by fanciers and for general purposes are no more valuable than the short haired ones, are not as hardy and are more trouble to handle as their coat needs careful attention.

Abyssinian.

This, like the Peruvian, is also a fancy breed. It has longer hair than the short-haired, and it stands out in curious little rosettes. These are more hardy than the Peruvian and are more common.

The Kind to Raise.

If you expect to raise Cavies for commercial purposes the English is the kind that should pay you best. They are easier to take care of than the long-haired varieties. For laboratories, experimental purposes, etc., it is the smooth-haired Cavy that is in most demand. If you are a Guinea Pig fancier or are raising them for pet purposes it is merely a matter of taste and choice. The long-haired ones are usually more expensive and sell for more, as they are scarcer and are generally sold for pet and fancy purposes. It is usually well to have a few Abyssinian among your stock if you are raising many, as many people prefer them for pets.

CHAPTER III

USES OF GUINEA PIGS.

There are three main uses to which Guinea Pigs are put, as food, as pets and for experimental purposes in laboratory and medical research. By far the largest demand is in the last named field.

Scientific Uses.

There is possibly no animal so well adapted for scientific experiments as the Guinea Pig. In the testing and analyzing of serums and antitoxins and for experimental purposes generally the demand is enormous, thousands and thousands of them being used every year. Many of the large hospitals and laboratories have been compelled to establish breeding pens of their own in order to be sure of a constant supply. The demand here is steadily increasing and many more would be used if they could be obtained at a reasonable price. A United States Bulletin says, "Guinea Pigs sell at various prices dependant on supply and demand. The average price for several years has been about 75c, but laboratories now report that suitable stock is short and that they have been paying from $1.00 to $1.50 for their supply of animals." For these purposes they are used all the way from nine weeks to six months or more old or when they weigh from 9 ounces and up. The cost of rearing them to this age is very little and a good profit is therefore assured the raiser.

As Pets.

The demand for Guinea Pigs as pets is very large. They are so widely used in the medical field that the pet stores have a hard time keeping enough on hand to supply the local demand for pets. They are very interesting and perfectly harmless little animals. They do not bite or scratch and young children can play with them. They are not as common as the ordinary pet, and being more of a novelty, attract more attention. When sold as pets they usually bring more than when sold to the hospitals and raisers are assured of a very large demand for this purpose. In England and Europe the Guinea Pig is more widely raised than in America and there are more fanciers who show and exhibit them extensively. They are becoming more popular in this country and are being exhibited more and more in Pet Stock Shows. A good show animal is worth all the way from $10 to $100. As a hobby the raising of Guinea Pigs is most interesting and instructive as there are so many experiments that can be made in the breeding.

As Food.

For food purposes Guinea Pigs are admirable, although not many are eaten in this country at the present time. However, many of the newspapers and magazines have run articles suggesting that they be raised for this purpose and there is really no reason why they should not be. The United States Government indorses them as food animals

English Cavies

and advises that they be used in this connection. In a few years we will possibly see Guinea Pigs sold in the stores as rabbits and poultry are now. Certainly no animal could be cleaner and being a vegetarian exclusively, its flesh is of the best. They can be prepared just as a rabbit or squirrel. In soups, stews, pies, or roasted, broiled or baked the young Cavy is equal to any other animal. For this purpose the animal should be about one-half grown.

CHAPTER IV

FOOD AND FEEDING.

The feeding of Guinea Pigs is a very simple matter. Their main food is good hay or dried grass. This should be before them all the time, as they will not eat too much of it. Be sure, however, that it is not musty or mouldy.

In addition to hay, they should have at least once a day, a feeding of green food. This is essential in keeping them from becoming constipated. By green food we mean such things as lawn clippings, green clover, spinach, green corn stalks, lettuce, celery tops, plantain, dandelion, grasses, etc., which is, of course, very plentiful in the summer. In the winter when you cannot get these, carrots, beets, apples, cabbage, mangle beets, yellow turnips, etc., will take their place.

The grains such as oats, wheat, corn, bran, chops, etc., should be fed them, as it makes flesh and gives them strength. Oats is probably the best of them all. Stale bread is also good, but it should not be greasy or mouldy. A good plan is to feed in the morning hay and grain or a bran or chops mash instead of the grain. At noon some green stuff or roots and at night hay. Give them all the hay they can eat. Keep it before them all of the time, but only feed as much green stuff as they can clear up in a few hours. They are also not apt to overeat grain, which should be fed in an earthern or wooden vessel. If you feed only twice a day, give them the green food in the morning with the hay. Guinea Pigs drink but little water when eating green food, but they should have a vessel of fresh water in the hutch or pen every morning. It is also well to keep a piece of rock salt in each hutch.

In the spring or summer you can feed more green stuff than in the winter, in fact, we have raised them in the summer on an exclusive green food diet by moving the hutches from place to place on the lawn. But in the winter and fall, when greens are scarce and they are not used to them, a sudden over-feeding might result in severe loss. Avoid a sudden change of diet.

In the spring and summer there is but little food to buy for them. Even the city raiser, by saving his own and his neighbors' lawn clippings, can be well supplied. By curing these clippings a good grade of hay is obtained. A little grain, especially for the pregnant mothers, is all that need be bought.

Bread and milk is a good flesh producer and should be fed any weak ones, also nursing mothers. In the winter it should be warmed.

The feeding of Cavies, you see, is a very simple matter, even for a city man. The commission houses every day throw away enough lettuce, cabbage, celery, etc., to feed a large number. Stale bread can always be bought very cheaply from the bakeries. On the farm nothing whatever need be bought at any time.

Doubtful Foods.

Breeders differ so as to doubtful foods that it is hard to advise what not to use. We get good results from alfalfa, but some breeders say it is too rich and gives them kidney trouble. We feed alfalfa hay in the winter with good results, but have had but little experience with it green. We would advise you to go light on it, however. Many breeders feed cabbage, while others say not. All are agreed, however, that potatoes, white turnips and parsnips are to be avoided. Of course, meat or greasy food must not be fed.

CHAPTER V

HOUSING.

Guinea Pigs do not require either large or elaborate quarters and the average man or boy can easily prepare a suitable place for them. There are two methods of housing usually used, namely, hutches and pens.

Hutches.

Among breeders generally the hutch method is

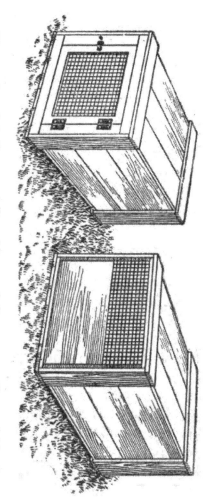

Figures 1 and 2. Front and Rear Views of Government Type of Hutch

preferred. They occupy less room, are easier to keep warm in the winter, and are easier handled. We illustrate several types. Fig. 1 and Fig. 2 are the kind used by the U. S. Department of Agriculture in the Bureau of Animal Industry. They are about 20 inches wide, 3½ feet deep and 18 inches high. They will accommodate a male and three or four females and young ones until weaned.

The door covers nearly the whole front and is made of wire netting. In the back is a screened opening for ventilation. Each hutch should have a shelf about four inches high in the back as they like to get on and under it. These hutches are made to stack one on another to utilize small space and are kept indoors.

Fig. 3 shows a type of hutch that can be built against the side of the wall. It is not best to have the wall of the house serve as the back of the hutch, it might be too cold. These can be built in tiers of three, each tier about 18 inches or two feet high. The size of each hutch can vary, depending on the number of Guinea Pigs you have. The entire front should be of wire with large doors so as to allow ventilation and to be easily cleaned. In the winter a small box can be put in each one for sleeping quarters and this box kept full of straw.

Pens.

Some breeders prefer pens and the pen system does have some advantages. In the first place, it gives the animals more room, has to be cleaned out less frequently and is more economical.

If you have a suitable place for making pens it will be all right to use them. Of course, it is harder to protect them from cats, rats and dogs in pens, and it is also harder to keep them warm in winter. In summer the pens are really to be preferred. If you have space in a barn, wood shed, attic, basement or any place that is protected from wind and rain and cats, rats and dogs, you can easily fix up a place for them. A place six by ten feet will accommodate from 30 to 50 Guinea Pigs. Your space should be divided into several different pens with 12 to 18 inch board or wire netting. Guinea Pigs do not burrow, so a board floor is not necessary. The floor should be covered with litter of some sort. Saw dust is good for a bottom layer. Hay or straw can be put on the saw dust. In the winter, if the place is not heated, boxes with a small hole for them to run in and out of and which should be filled with hay or straw, should be supplied for sleeping quarters.

Heat in the winter is not considered necessary by many very successful breeders, but we think it best they should have some protection, especially in very bitter weather, and the warmer you can keep them the better. They thrive better when the temperature does not fall below freezing. If given well protected, tight quarters with plenty of bedding they will get by all right without heat. However, the females that are about to litter should be kept in a warm place, as the little ones will freeze if the weather is very cold. After they get about a month old, you can, during a warm spell, move them out with the others. One of the most successful breeders in the West, whose stock brings fancy prices, opposes artificial heat and says they are better without it. Other breeders use oil stoves in the severe weather and some of the largest Caviaries have elaborate heating arrangements.

Out Door Hutches.

In the summer you can build a pen of wire netting for them to run in with a small tight box for sleeping quarters and protection from storm. Use small mesh chicken wire for the sides. The top can be of netting or boards. The size of the pen will of course depend on how many Cavies you have. These pens can be moved from place to place on the lawn, giving them good green grass. Very little other food then will be required.

General Instructions.

Give your stock all the room you can spare. Do not see how little room you can use, if you have room to waste. Be sure that they have ventilation, even in the winter. Animals, like humans, need fresh air. See that your hutches are kept clean and dry. Do not let your Cavies get wet. There is no need to build expensive and elaborate hutches, especially at the start. When you get a larger herd you can decide on some uniform style of hutch or pen and make them all alike. This makes them easy to handle and enlarge. Local conditions and circumstances will determine how you will keep your Cavies.

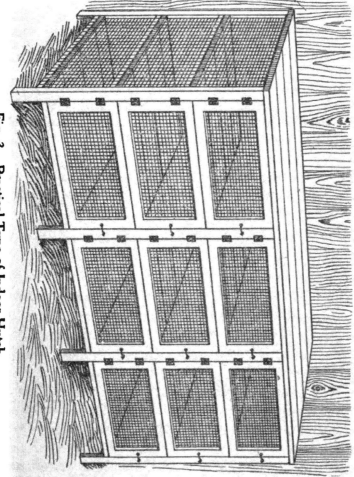

Fig. 3. Practical Type of Indoor Hutch.

CHAPTER VI

BREEDING.

Guinea Pigs are very prolific, having about five litters a year, and from two to five at a litter. Three is a safe average.

The females are sexually mature at a month, but, of course, should not be bred at that age. Three months is plenty early enough and some breeders wait until they are even older.

The period of gestation is from 65 to 70 days. The young ones are fully developed when born and in a few hours are able to run around. They begin eating other food in a day or two.

They should be weaned when about three weeks old and placed in separate pens, separating the young males from the females. It is then well to let the mother rest two or three weeks before being placed in the breeding pen again.

It is best to let each female have not over four litters a year. The young ones are apt to be stronger and there will be more of them in a litter. You will get about as many of them per year with four litters as with five and have better stock. Some breeders, especially for show stock, get only three litters a year.

When your young females are about four months old, they should be placed in the breeding pen. Best results and surer are obtained by keeping one male with four or five females and letting them stay together until you are sure each female is bred. They begin to show that they are with young in about 30 days or sooner and get to be very large before giving birth.

It is best to have several females with young together in the same pen, as they will nurse each other's young indiscriminately and the little fellows seem to know no difference. While the males do not kill the little ones, still they should never be left in the pen with nursing mothers, as they will bother them.

Many breeders do not have special breeding pens, but keep all of the females together and put males in with them. This is hardly the best plan, however. The females must not be allowed to litter in the big pen, but always in special pens or hutches.

It is best to have different breeding pens or hutches, so you can get young stock that is unrelated. You will have many chances to sell breeding stock and it does not do to supply males and females that are full brother and sister. By using care you can so breed your stock that you can keep different batches of them that are not very closely related.

Line Breeding.

By line breeding, we mean breeding the same stock without getting new males. It is the method used by breeders of fancy stock to get any special color or marking. It is not inbreeding in the true sense of the word.

In line breeding you breed the father to his daughter and the son to his mother. This arrange-

ment is all right and gets splendid results. You
must avoid, however, breeding full brothers and sis-
ters. It is also well to breed pigs that are similar
in color and marking. For instance: Breed whites
with whites and blacks with blacks, etc. By line
breeding you can get almost any color you want.
If you wanted to get solid red, say, out of a mixed
lot, you should breed your reddest male to your
reddest female. Then breed the father to his reddest daughter and the reddest son to his mother.
Continue in this way and eventually you will get
solid reds.

For commercial purposes, however, we think it
is best to get new males every now and then. If you
have only one male at the start, you should get a
new one when the young ones of your first litter are
old enough to breed. This will permit you to get
stock not closely related and that you can sell for
breeding and pet purposes.

It is best to breed males and females of different
ages. Have one older than the other. The females
should not be handled too much when they are with
young, as it is apt to injure them, and, of course,
no animal thrives as well when fondled. Always
keep your strongest and best males for breeders.

Too frequent littering tends to weaken both the
mother and the little ones. If you have a female
that gives weak young that are dead at birth or die
soon after, give her a rest of several months before
breeding her again. It is best to have fewer litters
and stronger stock.

The old males will sometimes fight when in the

pen together, but it is seldom that the females do not get along well together. If you have a fighting male keep him in a place to himself, as he is apt to injure the other males.

Good young breeding stock is to be preferred by one beginning to raise Cavies, because they have a longer life before them and if you get old stock you cannot tell how old they are. Guinea Pigs live to be about seven or eight years old and if you buy young stock you have them for their entire breeding age.

CHAPTER VII

EXHIBITING CAVIES.

The showing or exhibiting of Guinea Pigs is rapidly becoming more popular and in nearly all pet stock and poultry shows you will find several pens of Guinea Pigs. There are many fanciers in the country who make a specialty of show animals and fancy stock.

In judging Cavies, the size, shape, condition, and color are the main things to take into consideration. The selfs or solid colors must have every hair of the same color. Any white whatever will disbar a pig that is otherwise red. In the broken colors the different patches should be uniform in size and the colors not run into each other. Fancy stock is nearly always line bred and great pains should be taken in breeding. To secure the best stock the females are only bred twice or three times a year and every care is taken of them from birth. They are bred for size, shape and color. Even if you are not breeding for fancy stock, it will often pay you to enter your best specimens in local poultry and pet stock shows, as it gives you some good advertising and you will often take good prizes. It lets people know you have stock and you can always get good prices for your prize winners. Always enter as near a uniform lot as possible in singles, pairs or trios, or even larger pens.

While it costs more to produce fancy stock, still the higher prices you can get for it makes it pay. If you are raising only comparatively few pigs it might pay you to go in for fancy stock. Even if you have a large stock you can keep a few of your best specimens separate and give them little better attention.

Of course, many of the large commercial raisers never bother about fancy stock as it does not pay when you are raising large numbers of them.

Most of the shows are under the auspices of some pet stock association and a book of the standards can be secured from the secretary. We are giving below some of the classes under which stock is shown.

Selfs.

Solid colors throughout with no odd colored hairs.

Tortoise Shells.

Black and red colors with patches clear and distinct and as nearly as possible equal in size.

Tortoise and White.

Red, black and white patches, each clear cut with no running in of colors. The more patches and the more uniform in size the better.

Dutch Marked.

Blazed face of wedge shape. A band of white straight hair around the middle with no blending of colors. Feet white. Very rare.

Brindle.

Red and black evenly intermixed and perfectly brindled.

Agouti.

They are two shades, golden and gray. The golden should be rich brown undercolor with even ticking and belly of deep red. The gray should be a light shade with even ticking and belly of silver hue.

The eyes of all English Cavies should be large and bold. Head and shoulders heavy, nose roman, ears drooping.

In the Abyssinians the rosettes should be as plentiful as possible and the coat rough and wiry.

In the Peruvian the main thing to be considered is the length and silkiness of the coat.

A book giving the standards as adopted by the National Pet Stock Association of America can be obtained for 50c from its secretary, C. S. Gibson, 1045 W. Warren Ave., Detroit, Mich.

CHAPTER VIII

SELLING AND SHIPPING.

Guinea Pigs are in such wide demand that it is not a hard matter to sell them if you let people know you have them. There are dealers in various sections of the country that buy in wholesale lots but the prices obtained are usually not so high as if you find your own customers and develop your own trade.

The hospitals, medical colleges, agricultural schools, veterinary colleges, laboratories, pet stores, etc., are the heaviest users. You can get in touch with them by writing them and telling them you have Guinea Pigs for sale. The names of the hospitals and medical colleges can be gotten from any doctor and you, of course, know your own state University and Agricultural College.

Prices obtained for stock for experimental purposes are not as high as when they are sold for pets and breeding purposes. You can build up a good mail order business by putting a small classified advertisement in the poultry and pet stock columns in the Sunday issue of some large city newspaper near you. A classified ad in some of the poultry papers or farm papers in your state will usually find you good customers.

In shipping to hospitals and laboratories always send your males first and keep the females as when selling breeding stock you always have calls for more females than males.

The prices you get, of course depend on circumstances. 50c is a fair price for the general run of stock for experimental purposes. For pets and breeding purposes you should get from $1.50 per pair and up. Prices depend on supply and demand. $1.00 for females and 50c for males enable you to make a good profit with them.

For experimental purposes they are usually sold by weight and are salable from 9 ounces and up or when they are around six weeks old.

Shipping.

Guinea Pigs ship very easily. They go by express. Use a light but strong box in the summer have plenty of ventilation. Wire netting on the top or sides of the box is good but slats and holes in the sides will do.

In the winter not so much ventilation is needed.

For food use plenty of hay together with some green food or carrots, beets, etc. No water is necessary. Do not ship out during a real cold spell in winter or a real hot spell in summer.

Do not have your box larger than necessary as it means added weight and at the same time do not have it so small that they are crowded all over each other.

CHAPTER IX

DISEASES.

Guinea Pigs are singularly free from disease and the breeder has little to fear along this line. Of course improper food, irregular feeding hours, poorly ventilated or exposed quarters will often cause trouble but it is almost an unknown thing for an epidemic to get in a herd and kill them off. As long as they are fed judiciously and their quarters are kept sweet and clean and well protected from wind, rain and snow, you will have little trouble. They are remarkably healthy little animals but of course will not stand neglect or improper care. Do your share and you will but seldom lose a Cavy.

Diarrhoea.

This is one of the most common troubles that a Cavy raiser has to contend with. Too much green food, mouldy and half cured hay and a sudden change of food is usually the cause. Give them plenty of good sweet hay and cut out the green food for a while. A small spoon of olive oil or a little castor oil is good to clean out the bowels.

Constipation.

Caused by not enough green food. This trouble is not apt to occur except in winter when greens are scarce. Give them apple parings, any green stuff you can get and a little olive oil. Always try and feed at least once a day a little green stuff and you will have no trouble.

Premature Birth.

Females are occasionally lost when giving birth prematurely to little ones and sometimes the young ones when born are so weak that they do not live long. This is caused by too frequent littering, by fright, over fatness or physical weakness. Over crowding in a cold drafty hutch in severe weather may so weaken the mother that she bears weak ones. Take especially good care of the pregnant females. Give them the choice food and the best quarters. Do not let them breed too often or start too young. Do not allow them to be handled or frightened.

Worms.

If a Guinea Pig is a good feeder and still does not grow, if he looks unhealthy and his coat is not glossy he may have worms. Give a half teaspoonful of any kind of worm medicine such as children use. Feed lightly and not at all until the medicine has taken effect.

Going Light.

Sometimes in spite of all you can do a Guinea Pig goes light. If the treatment for worms has no effect it may be tuberculosis. Separate at once from the others. Give special diet of milk and bread or bran and oats. If it does not get better destroy it as it does not pay to have such stock around.

Colds, Pneumonia.

When they have pneumonia there is usually no help for them. Cold, damp and drafty quarters are usually the cause. About the only thing to do is to move them to warmer quarters, give warm milk and a few drops of any good cold remedy that you may have in the house. As an ounce of prevention is worth a pound of cure you should use every care to see that they do not catch cold.

Lice.

Use any good insect powder or any poultry lice killer. Clean out the hutches or pens and disinfect with any good disinfectant. They are not often bothered if kept in good condition.

Wounds.

Males sometimes hurt each other in fights. Cleanse the wound with warm water, remove the hair around it with sharp scissors and apply any good healing salve.

Running at the Eyes.

This is often caused by a cold. Wash the eyes in a solution of boric acid that you can get any druggist to put up for you.

Paralysis.

Cavies sometimes have dragging of the hind limbs. Some say alfalfa will cause it, but it is usually from some disorder of the kidneys. Give about 25 drops of sweet spirits of nitre three times a day and rub the limbs with a good liniment. Feed carefully for several days and they will often get over it.

General Instructions.

It is much easier to keep Cavies well than to cure a sick one, therefore, try and prevent trouble. Sick ones should be separated from the others and placed in comfortable quarters. Feed only choice food. Keep their quarters clean, sweet and well ventilated. Give them all air and sun you can and all the room for exercise you can. Feed no mouldy, wet or half cured hay or grass. Do feed grass that is wet with dew or rain. Just give your Cavies half a chance and you will find that disease will bother your Caviary but little.

CHAPTER X

PROFITS IN CAVY RAISING.

This industry in America is in its infancy. There are in several sections of the country large Cavy farms but they raise nothing like enough to supply the demand. Either as a side line with only a dozen or two females or whether raised as a business, Guinea Pigs offer a safe, sure and pleasant method of making money.

There is no danger that the business will be overdone as the demand is growing much more rapidly than the supply and as the supply increases more will be used. The hospitals in most cases use them in preference to any other animal for experimental purposes but at this time they cannot get them in sufficient quantities. There is and always will be a great demand for them as pets. When the people get educated to the food value, this end of the industry will come in for its share. The present high cost of meat and the decreasing supply of cattle indicate that in a few years the people of this country will have to make other preparations for their fresh meat and the Cavy offers the solution to the meat problem. All of these facts make it plain that there is no danger of there getting to be too many Cavies.

Inexpensive to Keep.

The profits in raising Guinea Pigs are large. The price for them on the open market runs all the way from 50c to several dollars each. The cost of raising them to the age when they are to be sold differs, of course with conditions and circumstances. The man on the farm or in the small town who has access to plenty of food for them without paying for it of course, can raise them cheaper than the man in the city. Even in the city, however, very little has to be bought and that only in the winter time as in the summer lawn clippings and vegetables from the table will feed them and all that will have to be bought is some grain or hay. By saving and curing the lawn clippings there will be no need of buying hay. They are far more profitable than poultry as they not only cost less to feed and keep but are not subject to the diseases that make poultry raising so unprofitable. They occupy smaller space and are not dirty, noisy or objectionable in any way. Many large Poultry Farms have been turned into Caviaries as their owners have seen that it is easier to make money with Guinea Pigs than with chickens.

Easy to Raise.

Anyone with ordinary intelligence should be able to raise Guinea Pigs successfully. Women do especially well with them as they require less attention and work than chickens. Boys and girls find the raising of them not only a pleasure but profitable and it is a splendid occupation for them as it requires no hard or laborious work. Youngsters from 10 to 17 or 18 years old need a responsibility of some kind and the experience gained in the raising and selling of Guinea Pigs will be very valuable to them in addition to the money they will make. Parents will do well to give their children a chance to raise them. To start with Guinea Pigs does not require a large outlay of capital. By starting with just a few and by keeping the young females it does not take long to build up a herd of breeders that are valuable. As each female produces about 15 young a year and as these young are worth from 50c to several dollars each, you can readily see there is a big opportunity for profit.

Big Profits.

Suppose you begin with six females. In one year they should produce about 90 young and the young females of the first one or two litters should be producing before the end of the year. Therefore, it is pretty safe to assume that from the six females and their litters you should get every year about 120 pigs. If sold at a price of 50c each these six females would be producing about $60 a year. These figures will show you what 100 females should do.

Starting.

Almost anyone can start raising Guinea Pigs without having to make any very special preparations or a large investment. In any new business it is always best to start in a small way. From a dozen to 25 females will give you an opportunity to learn their habits and you can increase your quarters as your herd increases. It would not be advisable for anyone to start with 100 or more right at once unles he has especially good place for them and a plentiful supply of food. However, by beginning in a small way no risk is taken and you can learn the business as you go along, and you can get extra stock as you make preparation for it.

Selection of Stock.

You cannot be too careful in the selection of your stock. Get good healthy animals to start with as on them depends your success. Scrub Guinea Pigs will pay no better than scrub poultry or cattle. Those found in pet stores are frequently unfitted for breeding purposes as they may have been experimented on or the descendants of such animals. Hospitals are very careful of whom they buy and must be assured of the purity of the stock. Therefore, you cannot be too careful in the selection of your original stock. Just as no one would start a live stock farm with the cheapest animals that can be bought, so no one should start a Cavy farm with the cheapest Cavies that can be bought. There are many reliable dealers in the country who have good stock for sale. Buy of a well known breeder or dealer and you will have no trouble. Young breeders are to be preferred as they have a longer life before them and are more valuable.

From our own experience with Guinea Pigs we would advise anyone who is interested in this work to take up the raising of them. Whether you have only a few for making a little money on the side or a large number as a real business you will find them very profitable. Certainly a great deal of pleasure can be gotten out of it and there is a wide sale for all you raise. If you will follow the instructions laid down in this little book we do not believe you will have any trouble making a success of the work.

PIGS

...et and experimental pur-
...ber, age, size or sex supplied promptly.

When you have Guinea Pigs for sale, write
us, as we are always in the market. Quote
price, giving number, size and sex.

CAVIES DISTRIBUTING CO.

The World's Largest Dealers in Guinea Pigs

712 West 74th Street   KANSAS CITY, MO.

BELGIAN HARES   RABBITS
SQUAB PIGEONS

Write me your wants and I will supply you. My
White Kings are the most profitable squab breeders in
the world, raising squabs weighing from a pound to a
pound and a half. Mature quickly and always command
top price. I can supply mated pairs. Write me today
for particulars and price on pigeons, rabbits and Belgian
Hares.

EDWARD F. TOBENER

2828A Woodland Ave.   KANSAS CITY, MO.

Redmen Printing Co., Kansas City

CPSIA information can be obtained
at www.ICGtesting.com
Printed in the USA
BVHW040201180821
614683BV00011B/374